SPEECH OF MR. WEBSTER

ON

MR. CLAY'S RESOLUTIONS.

DELIVERED IN THE SENATE OF THE UNITED STATES, MARCH 7, 18

The VICE PRESIDENT. The resolutions submitted by the Senator from Kentucky were made the ecial order of the day at 12 o'clock. The Senator from Wisconsin (Mr. WALKER) has the floor.

MR. WALKER. Mr. President, this vast audience has not assembled to hear me; and there is but e man, in my opinion, who can assemble such an audience. They expect to hear him, and I feel it be my duty, as it is my pleasure, to give the floor, therefore, to the Senator from Massachusetts. nderstand it is immaterial to him upon which of these questions he speaks, and therefore I will not ove to postpone the special order.

Mr. WEBSTER. I beg to express my obligations to my friend from Wisconsin, (Mr. WALKER,) as ll as to my friend from New York, (Mr. SEWARD,) for their courtesy in allowing me to address the nate this morning.

Mr. President, I wish to speak to-day, not as a Massachusetts man, nor as a Northern man, but as American, and a member of the Senate of the United States. It is fortunate that there is a Senate the United States; a body, not yet moved from its propriety, not lost to a just sense of its own dig-y, and its own high responsibilities, and a body to which the country looks, with confidence, for se, moderate, patriotic, and healing counsels. It is not to be denied that we live in the midst of ong agitations, and are surrounded by very considerable dangers to our institutions and Government. e imprisoned winds are let loose. The East, the West, the North, and the stormy South, all com-e to throw the whole ocean into commotion, to toss its billows to the skies, and disclose its pro-ndest depths. I do not affect to regard myself, Mr. President, as holding, or as fit to hold, the lm in this combat with the political elements; but I have a duty to perform, and I mean to perform it th fidelity, not without a sense of surrounding dangers, but not without hope. I have a part to t, not for my own security or safety, for I am looking out for no fragment upon which to float away m the wreck, if wreck there must be, but for the good of the whole, and the preservation of all; d there is that, which will keep me to my duty during this struggle, whether the sun and the rs shall appear, or shall not appear, for many days. I speak to-day for the preservation of the ion. "Hear me for my cause." I speak to-day, out of a solicitous and anxious heart, for the resto-tion to the country of that quiet and that harmony, which make the blessings of this Union so rich d so dear to us all. These are the topics that I propose to myself to discuss; these are the motives, d the sole motives, that influence me in the wish to communicate my opinions to the Senate and the untry; and if I can do any thing, however little, for the promotion of these ends, I shall have ac-mplished all that I expect.

Mr. President, it may not be amiss to recur very briefly to the events which, equally sudden and traordinary, have brought the political condition of the country to what it now is. In May, 1846, e United States declared war against Mexico. Our armies, then on the frontiers, entered the pro-nces of that Republic, met and defeated all her troops, penetrated her mountain passes, and occu-ed her capital. The marine force of the United States took possession of her forts and her towns, the Atlantic and on the Pacific. In less than two years a treaty was negotiated, by which Mexico ded to the United States a vast territory, extending seven or eight hundred miles along the shores of e Pacific, and reaching back over the mountains, and across the desert, until it joined the frontier of e State of Texas. It so happened that, in the distracted and feeble state of the Mexican Govern-ent, before the declaration of war by the United States against Mexico had become known in Cali-rnia, the people of California, under the lead of American officers, overthrew the existing Provin-l Government of California, the Mexican authorities, and run up an independent flag. When e news arrived at St. Francisco that war had been declared by the United States against Mexico, is independent flag was pulled down and the stars and stripes of this Union hoisted in its stead. So, , before the war was over, the powers of the United States, military and naval, had possession of n Francisco and Upper California, and a great rush of emigrants from various parts of the world took ce into California in 1846 and 1847. But now, behold another wonder.

In January of 1848, the Mormons, or some of them, made a discovery of an extraordinarily h mine of gold, or, rather, of a very great quantity of gold, hardly fit to be called a mine, for it s spread near the surface, on the lower part of the South, or American, branch of the Sacramento. hey seem to have attempted to conceal their discovery for some time; but soon another discovery,

GIDEON & Co., Printers.

perhaps of greater importance, was made of gold, in another part of the American branch of the Sacramento, and near Sutter's fort, as it is called. The fame of these discoveries spread far and wide. They inflamed more and more the spirit of emigration towards California, which had already been excited; and persons crowded in hundreds, and flocked towards the bay of San Francisco. This, as I have said, took place in the winter and spring of 1848. The digging commenced in the spring of that year, and from that time to this the work of searching for gold has been prosecuted with a success not heretofore known in the history of this globe. We all know, sir, how incredulous the American public was at the accounts which reached us, at first, of these discoveries; but we all know, now, that these accounts received, and continue to receive, daily confirmation, and down to the present moment I suppose the assurances are as strong, after the experience of these several months, of mines of gold apparently inexhaustible in the regions near San Francisco, in California, as they were at any period of the earlier dates of the accounts. It so happened, sir, that, although after the return of peace, it became a very important subject for legislative consideration and legislative decision to provide a proper Territorial Government for California, yet differences of opinion in the counsels of the Government prevented the establishment of any such Territorial Government at the last session of Congress. Under this state of things, the inhabitants of San Francisco and California, then amounting to a great number of people; in the summer of last year, thought it to be their duty to establish a local Government. Under the proclamation of General Riley, the people chose delegates to a Convention; that Convention met at Monterey. They formed a constitution for the State of California, and it was adopted by the people of California in their primary assemblages. Desirous of immediate connexion with the United States, its Senators were appointed and Representatives chosen, who have come hither, bringing with them the authentic constitution of the State of California; and they now present themselves, asking, in behalf of their State, that it may be admitted into this Union as one of the United States. This constitution, sir, contains an express prohibition against slavery or involuntary servitude in the State of California. It is said, and I suppose truly, that of the members who composed that Convention some sixteen were natives, and had been residents, in the slaveholding States, about twenty-two were from the non-slaveholding States, and the remaining ten members were either native Californians or old settlers in that country. This prohibition against slavery, it is said, was inserted with entire unanimity.

Mr. Hale. Will the Senator give way until order is restored?

The Vice President. The Sergeant-at Arms will see that order is restored, and no more persons admitted to the floor.

Mr. Cass. I trust the scene of the other day will not be repeated. The Sergeant-at-Arms must display more energy in suppressing this disorder.

Mr. Hale. The noise is outside of the door.

Mr. Webster. And it is this circumstance, sir, the prohibition of slavery by that convention, which has contributed to raise, I do not say it has wholly raised, the dispute as to the propriety of the admission of California into the Union under this constitution. It is not to be denied, Mr. President, nobody thinks of denying, that, whatever reasons were assigned at the commencement of the late war with Mexico, it was prosecuted for the purpose of the acquisition of territory, and under the alleged argument that the cession of territory was the only form in which proper compensation could be made to the United States by Mexico for the various claims and demands, which the people of this country had against that government. At any rate, it will be found that President Polk's message at the commencement of the session of December, 1847, avowed that the war was to be prosecuted until some acquisition of territory should be made. And, as the acquisition was to be south of the line of the United States, in warm climates and countries, it was naturally, I suppose, expected by the South, that whatever acquisitions were made in that region would be added to the slaveholding portion of the United States. Events have turned out as was not expected, and that expectation has not been realized; and therefore some degree of disappointment and surprise has resulted. In other words, it is obvious that the question which has so long harrassed the country, and at some times very seriously alarmed the minds of wise and good men, has come upon us for a fresh discussion, the question of slavery in these United States.

Now, sir, I propose, perhaps at the expense of some detail and consequent detention of the Senate, to review historically this question of slavery, which, partly in consequence of its own importance, and partly, perhaps mostly, in consequence of the manner in which it has been discussed in one and the other portion of the country, has been a source of so much alienation and unkind feeling between the different portions of the Union.

We all know, sir, that slavery has existed in the world from time immemorial. There was slavery, in the earliest periods of history, in the Oriental nations. There was slavery among the Jews; the theocratic government of that people ordained no injunction against it. There was slavery among the Greeks; and the ingenious philosophy of the Greeks found, or sought to find, a justification for it exactly upon the grounds which have been assumed for such a justification in this country; that is a natural and original difference among the races of mankind, and the inferiority of the black or colored race, to the white. The Greeks justified their system of slavery upon that ground precisely. They held the African, and in some parts the Asiatic, tribes to be inferior to the white race; but they did not show, I think, by any close process of logic, that, if this were true, the more intelligent and the stronger had therefore a right to subjugate the weaker.

The more manly philosophy and jurisprudence of the Romans placed the justification of slavery on entirely different grounds.

The Roman jurists, from the first and down to the fall of the empire, admitted that slavery was against the natural law, by which, as they maintained, all men, of whatsoever clime, color, or capacity, were equal; but they justified slavery, first, upon the ground and authority of the law of nations, arguing, and arguing truly, that at that day the conventional law of nations admitted that captives in war, whose lives, according to the notions of the times, were at the absolute disposal of the captors, might, in exchange for exemption from death, be made slaves for life, and that such servitude might descend to their posterity. The jurists of Rome also maintained that by the civil law there might be servitude or slavery, personal and hereditary; first, by the voluntary act of an individual who might sell himself into slavery; second, by his being received into a state of slavery by his creditors in satisfaction of a debt; and, thirdly, by being placed in a state of servitude or slavery for crime. At the introduction of Christianity, the Roman world was full of slaves, and I suppose there is to be found no injunction against that relation between man and man, in the teachings of the Gospel of Jesus Christ, or of any of his Apostles. The object of the instruction imparted to mankind by the founder of Christianity was to touch the heart, purify the soul, and improve the lives of individual men. That object went directly to the first fountain of all political and all social relations of the human race, as well as of all true religious feeling, the individual heart and mind of man.

Now, sir, upon the general nature, and character and influence of slavery, there exists a wide difference between the Northern portion of this country and the Southern. It is said on the one side that, if not the subject of any injunction or direct prohibition in the New Testament, slavery is a wrong; that it is founded merely in the right of the strongest; and that it is an oppression, like unjust wars, like all those conflicts by which a mighty nation subjects a weaker nation to its will; and that slavery, in its nature, whatever may be said of it in the modifications which have taken place, is not in fact according to the meek spirit of the Gospel. It is not kindly affectioned; it does not "seek another's and not its own." It does not "let the oppressed go free." These are sentiments that are cherished, and recently with greatly augmented force, among the people of the Northern States. It has taken hold of the religious sentiment of that part of the country, as it has more or less taken hold of the religious feelings of a considerable portion of mankind. The South, upon the other side, having been accustomed to this relation between the two races all their lives, from their birth; having been taught, in general, to treat the subjects of this bondage with care and kindness, and I believe, in general, feeling for them great care and kindness, have not taken this view of the subject which I have mentioned. There are thousands of religious men, with consciences as tender as any of their brethren at the North, who do not see the unlawfulness of slavery; and there are more thousands perhaps that, whatsoever they may think of it in its origin, and as a matter depending upon natural right, yet take things as they are, and, finding slavery to be an established relation of the society in which they live, can see no way in which, let their opinions on the abstract question be what they may, it is in the power of the present generation to relieve themselves from this relation. And, in this respect, candor obliges me to say, that I believe they are just as conscientious, many of them, and the religious people all of them, as they are in the North in holding different opinions.

Why, sir, the honorable Senator from South Carolina, the other day, alluded to the separation of that great religious community, the Methodist Episcopal Church. That separation was brought about by differences of opinion upon this particular subject of slavery. I felt great concern, as that dispute went on, about the result, and I was in hopes that the difference of opinion might be adjusted, because I looked upon that religious denomination as one of the great props of religion and morals, throughout the whole country, from Maine to Georgia. The result was against my wishes and against my hopes. I have read all their proceedings, and all their arguments, but I have never yet been able to come to the conclusion that there was any real ground for that separation; in other words, that no good could be produced by that separation. I must say I think there was some want of candor and charity. Sir, when a question of this kind takes hold of the religious sentiments of mankind, and comes to be discussed in religious assemblies of the clergy and laity, there is always to be expected, or always to be feared, a great degree of excitement. It is in the nature of man, manifested by his whole history, that religious disputes are apt to become warm, as men's strength of conviction is proportionate to their views of the magnitude of the questions. In all such disputes there will sometimes men be found with whom every thing is absolute, absolutely wrong, or absolutely right. They see the right clearly; they think others ought so to see it, and they are disposed to establish a broad line of distinction between what is right and what is wrong. And they are not seldom willing to establish that line upon their own convictions of truth and justice; and are willing to mark and guard that line, by placing along it a series of dogmas, as lines of boundary are marked by posts and stones. There are men who, with clear perceptions, as they think, of their own duty, do not see how too hot a pursuit of one duty may involve them in the violation of others, or how too warm an embracement of one truth may lead to a disregard of other truths equally important. As I heard it stated strongly, not many days ago, these persons are disposed to mount upon some particular duty as upon a war horse, and to drive furiously, on and upon, and over all other duties that may stand in the way. There are men who, in times of that sort, and in disputes of that sort, are of opinion that human duties may be ascertained with the exactness of mathematics. They deal with morals as with mathematics, and they think what is right may be distinguished from what is wrong with the precision of an algebraic equation. They have, therefore, none too much charity towards others who differ from them. They are apt, too, to think that nothing is good but what is perfect, and that there are no compromises or modifications to be made in submission to difference of opinion, or in deference to other men's judgment. If their perspicacious vision enables them to detect a spot on the face of the sun, they think that a good reason why the sun should be struck down from heaven. They prefer the chance of running into utter darkness, to living in heavenly light, if that heavenly light be not absolutely without any imperfection. There are impatient men, too impatient always to give heed to the admonition of St. Paul, "that we are not to do evil that good may come;" too impatient to wait for the slow progress of moral causes in the improvement of mankind. They do not remember, that the doctrines and the miracles of Jesus Christ have, in eighteen hundred years, converted only a small portion of the human race; and among the nations that are converted to Christianity, they forget how many vices and crimes, public and private, still prevail, and that many of them, public crimes especially, which are offences against the Christian religion, pass without exciting particular indignation. Thus wars are waged, and unjust wars. I do not deny that there may be just wars. There certainly are, but it was the remark of an eminent person, not many years ago, on the other side of the Atlantic, that it was one of the greatest reproaches to human nature that wars were sometimes just. The defence of nations sometimes causes a just war against the injustice of other nations.

Now, sir, in this state of sentiment upon the general nature of slavery lies the cause of a great portion of those unhappy divisions, exasperations, and reproaches which find vent and support in different parts of the Union. Slavery does exist in the United States. It did exist in the States before the adoption of this Constitution, and at that time.

And now let us consider, sir, for a moment, what was the state of sentiment, north and south, in regard to slavery, at the time this Constitution was adopted. A remarkable change has taken place since, but what did the wise and great men of all parts of the country think of slavery, then? In what estimation did they hold it at the time, when this Constitution was adopted? Now, it will be found, sir, if we will carry ourselves by historical research back to that day, and ascertain men's opinions by authentic records still existing among us, that there was no great diversity of opinion between the North and the South upon the subject of slavery, and it will be found that both parts of the country held it equally an evil, a moral and political evil. It will not be found, that either at the North or at the South there was much, though there was some, invective against slavery as inhuman and cruel. The great ground of objection to it was political; that it weakened the social fabric; that, taking the place of free labor, society became less strong and labor was less productive; and therefore we find from all the eminent men of the time the clearest expression of their opinion that slavery was an evil. And they ascribed its existence here, not without truth, and not without some acerbity of temper and force of language, to the injurious policy of the mother country, who, to favor the navigator, had entailed these evils upon the colonies. I need hardly refer, sir, to the publications of the day. They are matters of history on the record. The eminent men, the most eminent men and nearly all the conspicuous politicians of the South, held the same sentiments; that slavery was an evil, a blight, a blast, a mildew, a scourge, and a curse. There are no terms of reprobation of slavery so vehement in the North of that day as in the South. The North was not so much excited against it as the South; and the reason is, I suppose, because there was much less of it at the North, and the people did not see, or think they saw, the evils so prominently as they were seen, or thought to be seen, at the South.

Then, sir, when this Constitution was framed, this was the light in which the Convention viewed it. The Convention reflected the judgment and sentiments of the great men of the South. A member of the other House, whom I have not the honor to know, in a recent speech, has collected extracts from these public documents. They prove the truth of what I am saying, and the question then was, how to deal with it, and how to deal with it as an evil? Well, they came to this general result. They thought that slavery could not be continued in the country, if the importation of slaves were made to cease, and therefore they provided that after a certain period the importation might be prevented by the act of the new Government. Twenty years was proposed by some gentleman, a Northern gentleman, I think, and many of the Southern gentlemen opposed it as being too long. Mr. Madison especially was something warm against it. He said it would bring too much of this mischief into the country to allow the importation of slaves for such a period. Because we must take along with us, in the whole of this discussion, when we are considering the sentiments and opinions in which this constitutional provision originated, that the conviction of all men was, that if the importation of slaves ceased, the white race would multiply faster than the black race, and that slavery would therefore gradually wear out and expire. It may not be improper here to allude to that, I had almost said, celebrated opinion of Mr. Madison. You observe, sir, that the term slave or slavery is not used in the Constitution. The Constitution does not require that "fugitive slaves" shall be delivered up. It requires that "persons bound to service in one State, and escaping into another, shall be delivered up." Mr. Madison opposed the introduction of the term slave or slavery into the Constitution; for he said, that he did not wish to see it recognised by the Constitution of the United States of America that there could be property in men. Now, sir, all this took place at the Convention in 1787; but connected with this, concurrent and contemporaneous, is another important transaction not sufficiently attended to. The Convention for framing this Constitution assembled in Philadelphia in May, and sat until September, 1787. During all that time the Congress of the United States was in session at New York. It was a matter of design, as we know, that the Convention should not assemble in the same city where Congress was holding its sessions. Almost all the public men of the country, therefore, of distinction and eminence, were in one or the other of these two assemblies; and I think it happened in some instances that the same gentlemen were members of both. If I mistake not, such was the case of Mr. Rufus King, then a member of Congress from Massachusetts, and at the same time a member of the Convention to frame the Constitution, from that State. Now, it was in the summer of 1787, the very time when the Convention in Philadelphia was framing this Constitution, that the Congress in New York was framing the ordinance of 1787. They passed that ordinance on the 13th July, 1787, at New York, the very month, perhaps the very day, on which these questions about the importation of slaves and the character of slavery were debated in the Convention at Philadelphia. And, so far as we can now learn, there was a perfect concurrence of opinion between these respective bodies; and it resulted in this ordinance of 1787, excluding slavery as applied to all the territory over which the Congress of the United States had jurisdiction, and that was, all the territory northwest of the Ohio. Three years before, Virginia and other States had made a cession of that great territory to the United States. And a most magnificent act it was. I never reflect upon it without a disposition to do honor and justice, and justice would be the highest honor, to Virginia, for the cession of her northwestern territory. I will say, sir, it is one of her fairest claims to the respect and gratitude of the United States, and that perhaps it is only second to that other claim which attaches to her; that, from her counsels, and from the intelligence and patriotism of her leading statesmen, proceeded the first idea put into practice of the formation of a general constitution of the United States. Now, sir, the ordinance of 1787 applied thus to the whole territory over which the Congress of the United States had jurisdiction. It was adopted nearly three years before the Constitution of the United States went into operation; because the ordinance took effect immediately on its passage, while the Constitution of the United States, having been framed, was to be sent to the States to be adopted by their Conventions; and then a Government was to be organized under it. This ordinance, then, was in operation and force when the Constitution was adopted and this Government put in motion, in April, 1789.

Mr. President, three things are quite clear, as historical truths. One is, that there was an expectation that on the ceasing of the importation of slaves from Africa, slavery would begin to run out. That was hoped and expected. Another is, that as far as there was any power in Congress to prevent the spread of slavery in the United States, that power was executed in the most absolute manner and to the fullest extent. An honorable member whose health does not allow him to be here to-day—

A SENATOR. He is here. (Referring to Mr. CALHOUN.)

Mr. WEBSTER. I am very happy to hear that he is; may he long be here, and in the enjoyment of health to serve his country! The honorable member said the other day, that he considered this ordinance as the first, in the series of measures, calculated to enfeeble the South and deprive them of their just participation in the benefits and privileges of this Government. He says very properly that it was done under the old confederation and before this Constitution went into effect; but, my present purpose is only to say, Mr. President, that it was established with the entire and unanimous concurrence of the whole South. Why, there it stands! The vote of every State in the Union was unanimous in favor of the ordinance, with the exception of a single individual vote, and that individual vote was given by a Northern man. But, sir, the ordinance abolishing, or rather prohibiting, slavery northwest of the Ohio, has the hand and seal of every Southern member in Congress. The other and third clear historical truth is, that the Convention meant to leave slavery, in the States, as they found it, entirely under the authority and control of the States.

This was the state of things, sir, and this the state of opinion, under which those very important matters were arranged, and those three important things done; that is, the establishment of the Constitution with a recognition of slavery as it existed in the States, the establishment of the ordinance prohibiting to the full extent of all territory owned by the United States, the introduction of slavery into those territories, and the leaving to the States of all power over slavery, in their own limits. And here, sir, we may pause. We may reflect for a moment upon the entire coincidence and concurrence of sentiment, between the North and the South, upon those questions, at the period of the adoption of the Constitution. But opinions, sir, have changed, greatly changed, changed North, and changed South. Slavery is not regarded in the South now, as it was then. I see an honorable member of this body paying me the honor of listening to my remarks; he brings to me, sir, freshly and vividly the sentiments of his great ancestor, so much distinguished in his day and generation, so worthy to be succeeded by so worthy a grandson, with all the sentiments he expressed in the Convention in Philadelphia.

Here we may pause. There was, if not an entire unanimity, a general concurrence of sentiment, running through the whole community, and especially entertained by the eminent men of all parts of the country. But soon a change began, at the North and the South, and a severance of opinion showed itself, the North growing much more warm and strong against slavery, and the South growing much more warm and strong in its support. Sir, there is no generation of mankind whose opinions are not subject to be influenced by what appears to them to be their present, emergent, and exigent interest. I impute to the South no particularly selfish view in the change which has come over her. I impute to her certainly no dishonest view. All that has happened has been natural. It has followed those causes which always influence the human mind and operate upon it. What, then, have been the causes which have created so new a feeling in favor of slavery in the South, which have changed the whole nomenclature of the South on that subject, so that, from being thought and described in the terms I have mentioned and will not repeat, it has now become an institution, a cherished institution, in that quarter; no evil, no scourge, but a great religious, social, and moral blessing, as I think I have heard it latterly spoken? I suppose this, sir, is owing to the sudden uprising and rapid growth of the cotton plantations of the South. So far as any motive consistent with honor, justice, and general judgment could act, it was the cotton interest that gave a new desire to promote slavery, to spread it and to use its labor. I again say that that was produced by causes which we must always expect to produce like effects; the whole interest of the South became connected, more or less, connected with it. If we look back to the history of the commerce of this country at the early years of this Government, what were our exports? Cotton was hardly, or but to a very limited extent, known. The tables will show that the exports of cotton for the years 1790 and '91 were not more than forty or fifty thousand dollars a year. It has gone on increasing rapidly, until it may now, perhaps, in a season of great product and high prices, amount to a hundred millions of dollars. In the years I have mentioned, there was more of wax, more of indigo, more of rice, more of almost every article of export from the South, than of cotton. I think I have heard it said, when Mr. Jay negotiated the treaty of 1794 with England, that he did not know that cotton was exported at all from the United States; and I have heard it said also that, after the treaty which gave to the United States the right to carry their own commodities to England in their own ships, the custom-house in London refused to admit cotton, upon an allegation that it could not be an American production, there being, as they supposed, no cotton raised in America. They would hardly think so now!

Well, sir, we know what followed. The age of cotton became the golden age for our Southern brethren. It gratified their desire for improvement and accumulation, at the same time that it excited it. The desire grew by what it fed upon, and there soon came to be an eagerness for other territory, a new area or new areas for the cultivation of the cotton crop; and measures leading to this result were brought about rapidly, one after another, under the lead of Southern men at the head of the Government, they having a majority in both branches to accomplish their ends. The honorable member from South Carolina observed that there has been a majority all along in favor of the North. If that be true, sir, the North has acted either very liberally and kindly, or very weakly; for they never exercised that majority efficiently five times in the history of the Government. Never. Whether they were out-generaled, or whether it was owing to other causes, I shall not stop to consider, but no man acquainted with the history of the country can deny, that the general lead in the politics of the country for three-fourths of the period that has elapsed since the adoption of the Constitution, has been a Southern lead. In 1802, in pursuit of the idea of opening a new cotton region, the United States obtained a cession from Georgia of the whole of her western territory, now embracing the rich and growing State of Alabama. In 1803, Louisiana was purchased from France, out of which the States of Louisiana, Arkansas, and Missouri have been framed, as slaveholding States. In 1819, the cession of Florida was made, bringing another cession of slaveholding property and territory. Sir, the honorable member from South Carolina thought he saw in certain operations of the Government, such as the manner of collecting the revenue and the tendency of those measures to promote emigration into the country, what accounts for the more rapid growth of the North than the South. He ascribes that more rapid growth, not to the operation of time, but to the system of government administration established under this Constitution. That is matter of opinion. To a certain extent it may be; but it does seem to me that if any operation of the Government could be shown in any degree to have promoted the population, and growth, and wealth of the North, it is much more sure that there are sundry important and distinct operations of the Government, about which no man can doubt, tending to promote, and which absolutely have promoted, the increase of the slave interest and the slave territory of the South. Allow me to say that it was not time that brought in Louisiana; it was the act of men. It was not time that brought in Florida; it was the act of men. And lastly, sir, to complete those acts of men which have contributed so much to enlarge the area and the sphere of the institution of slavery, Texas, great and vast and illimitable Texas, was added to the Union as a slave State in 1845; and that, sir, pretty much closed the whole chapter, and settled the whole account. That closed the whole chapter, that settled the whole account, because the annexation of Texas, upon the conditions and under the guaranties upon which she was admitted, did not leave within the control of this Government an acre of land, capable of being cultivated by slave labor, between this Capitol and the Rio Grande or the Nueces, or whatever is the proper boundary of Texas, not an acre. From that moment the whole country, from this place to the western boundary of Texas, was fixed, pledged, fastened, decided, to be slave territory forever, by the solemn guaranties of law. And I now say, sir, as the proposition upon which I stand this day, and upon the truth and firmness of which I intend to act until it is overthrown, that there is not at this moment within the United States, or any territory of the United States, a single foot of land, the character of which, in regard to its being free-soil territory or slave territory, is not fixed by some law, and some irrepealable law, beyond the power of the action of the Government. Now, is it not so with respect to Texas? Why, it is most manifestly so. The honorable member from South Carolina, at the time of the admission of Texas, held an important post in the Executive Department of the Government; he was Secretary of State. Another eminent person of great activity and adroitness in affairs, I mean the late Secretary of the Treasury, (Mr. Walker,) was an eminent member of this body, and took the lead in the business of annexation; and I must say that they did their business faithfully and thoroughly, there was no botch left in it. They rounded it off, and made as close joiner-work as ever was put together. Resolutions of annexation were brought into Congress fitly joined together, compact, firm, efficient, conclusive upon the great object which they had in view, and those resolutions passed.

Allow me to read a part of these resolutions. It is the third clause of the second section of the resolution of the 1st March, 1845, for the admission of Texas, which applies to this part of the case. That clause reads in these words:

"New States, of convenient size, not exceeding four in number, in addition to said State of Texas, and having sufficient population, may hereafter, by the consent of said State, be formed out of the Territory thereof, which shall be entitled to admission under the provisions of the Federal Constitution. And such States as may be formed out of that portion of said Territory lying south of thirty-six degrees thirty minutes north latitude, commonly known as the Missouri compromise line, shall be admitted into the Union with or without slavery, as the people of each State asking admission may desire; and in such State or States as shall be formed out of said Territory north of said Missouri compromise line, slavery or involuntary servitude (except for crime) shall be prohibited."

Now what is here stipulated, enacted, secured? It is, that all Texas south of 36° 30′, which is nearly the whole of it, shall be admitted into the Union as a slave State. It was a slave State, and therefore came in as a slave State; and the guaranty is, that new States shall be made out of it, and that such States as are formed out of that portion of Texas lying south of 36° 30′ may come in as slave States to the number of four, in addition to the State then in existence, and admitted at that time by these resolutions. I know no form of legislation which can strengthen that. I know no mode of recognition that can add a tittle of weight to it. I listened respectfully to the resolutions of my honorable friend from Tennessee, (Mr. Bell.) He proposed to recognise that stipulation with Texas. But any additional recognition would weaken the force of it; because it stands here on the ground of a contract, a thing done for a consideration. It is a law founded on a contract with Texas, and designed to carry that contract into effect. A recognition, now, founded not on any consideration or any contract would not be so strong as it now stands on the face of the resolution. Now I know no way, I candidly confess, in which this Government, acting in good faith, as I trust it always will, can relieve itself from that stipulation and pledge, by any honest course of legislation whatever. And, therefore, I say again that, so far as Texas is concerned, the whole of Texas south of 36° 30′, which I suppose embraces all the slave territory, there is no land, not an acre, the character of which is not established by law, a law which cannot be repealed without the violation of a contract, and plain disregard of the public faith.

I hope, sir, it is now apparent that my proposition, so far as Texas is concerned, has been maintained; and the provision in this article, and it has been well suggested by my friend from Rhode Island that that part of Texas which lies north of thirty-four degrees of north latitude may be formed into free States, is dependant, in like manner, upon the consent of Texas, herself a slave State.

Well, now, sir, how came this? How came it to pass, that within these walls, where it is said by the honorable member from South Carolina that the free States have a majority, this resolution of annexation, such as I have described it, found a majority in both Houses of Congress? Why, sir, it found that majority by the great number of Northern votes added to the entire Southern vote, or at least nearly the whole of the Southern votes. That majority was made up of Northern, as well as of Southern votes. In the House of Representatives it stood, I think, about eighty Southern votes for the admission of Texas, and about fifty Northern votes for the admission of Texas. In the Senate the vote stood for the admission of Texas twenty-seven, and twenty-five against it; and of those twenty-seven votes, constituting a majority for the admission of Texas in this body, no less than thirteen came from the free States, four of them were from New England. The whole of these thirteen Senators from the free States, within a fraction, you see, of one-half of all the votes in this body for the admission of Texas, with its immeasurable extent of slave territory, were sent here by free States.

Sir, there is not so remarkable a chapter in our history of political events, political parties, and political men, as is afforded by this measure for the admission of Texas, with this immense territory, that a bird cannot fly over in a week. [Laughter.] Sir, New England, with some of her own votes, supported this measure. Three-fourths of the votes of liberty-loving Connecticut were given for it in the other House, and one-half here. There was one vote for it in Maine, but I am happy to say not the vote of the honorable member who addressed the Senate the day before yesterday, (Mr. Hamlin,) and who was then a Representative from Maine in the other House; but there was a vote or two from Maine, aye, and there was one vote for it from Massachusetts, the gentleman then representing, and now living in, the district in which the prevalence of free-soil sentiment for a couple of years or so has defeated the choice of any member to represent it in Congress. Sir, that body of Northern and Eastern men, who gave those votes at that time, are now seen taking upon themselves, in the nomenclature of politics, the appellation of the Northern Democracy. They undertook to wield the destinies of this empire, if I may call a republic an empire, and their policy was, and they persisted in it, to bring into this country all the territory they could. They did it under pledges, absolute pledges to the slave interest in the case of Texas, and afterwards they lent their aid in bringing in these new conquests. My honorable friend from Georgia, in March, 1847, moved the Senate to declare that the war ought not to be prosecuted for acquisition, for conquest, for the dismemberment of Mexico. The same Northern Democracy entirely voted against it. He did not get a vote from them. It suited the views, the patriotism, the elevated sentiments of the Northern Democracy to bring in a world here, among the mountains and valleys of California and New Mexico, or any other part of Mexico, and then quarrel about it, to bring it in, and then endeavor to put upon it the saving grace of the Wilmot proviso. There were two eminent and highly respectable gentlemen from the North and East, then leading gentlemen in the Senate, I refer, and I do so with entire respect, for I entertain for both of those gentlemen, in general high regard, to Mr. Dix, of New York, and Mr. Niles, of Connecticut, who voted for the admission of Texas. They would not have that vote any other way than as it stood; and they would have it as it did stand. I speak of the vote upon the annexation of Texas. Those two gentlemen would have the resolution of annexation just as it is, and they voted for it just as it is, and their eyes were all open to it. The honorable member who addressed us the other day from South Carolina, was then Secretary of State. His correspondence with Mr. Murphy, the chargé d'affaires of the United States in Texas, had been published. That correspondence was all before those gentlemen, and the Secretary had the boldness and candor to avow in that correspondence that the great object sought by the annexation of Texas was to strengthen the slave interest of the South. Why, sir, he said, in so many words—

Mr. Calhoun. Will the honorable Senator permit me to interrupt him for a moment?

Mr. Webster. Certainly.

Mr. Calhoun. I am very reluctant to interrupt the honorable gentleman; but, upon a point of so much importance, I deem it right to put myself *rectus in curia*. I did not put it upon the ground assumed by the Senator. I put it upon this ground: that Great Britain had announced to this country, in so many words, that her object was to abolish slavery in Texas, and through Texas to accomplish the abolishment of slavery in the United States and the world. The ground I put it on was, that it would make an exposed frontier, and, if Great Britain succeeded in her object, it would be impossible that that frontier could be secured against the aggression of the abolitionists; and that this Government was bound, under the guaranties of the Constitution, to protect us against such a state of things.

Mr. Webster. That comes, I suppose, sir, to exactly the same thing. It was, that Texas must be obtained for the security of the slave interest of the South.

Mr. Calhoun. Another view is very distinctly given.

Mr. Webster. That was the object set forth in the correspondence of a worthy gentleman not now living, who preceded the honorable member from South Carolina in that office. There repose on the files of the Department of State, as I have occasion to know, strong letters from Mr. Upshur to the United States minister in England, and I believe there are some to the same minister from the honorable Senator himself, asserting to this effect the sentiments of this Government, that Great Britain was expected not to interfere to take Texas out of the hands of its then existing Government, and make it a free country. But my argument, my suggestion is this; that those gentlemen who composed the Northern Democracy when Texas was brought into the Union, saw, with all their eyes, that it was brought in as a slave country, and brought in for the purpose of being maintained as slave territory to the Greek Kalends. I rather think the honorable gentleman who was then Secretary of State might, in some of his correspondence with Mr. Murphy, have suggested that it was not expedient to say too much about this object, lest it should create some alarm. At any rate, Mr. Murphy wrote to him, that England was anxious to get rid of the constitution of Texas, because it was a constitution establishing slavery; and that what the United States had to do, was to aid the people of Texas in upholding their constitution; but that nothing should be said, which should offend the fanatical men of the North. But, sir, the honorable member did avow this object himself, openly, boldly, and manfully; he did not disguise his conduct, or his motives.

Mr. Calhoun. Never, never.

Mr. Webster. What he means he is very apt to say.

Mr. Calhoun. Always, always.

Mr. Webster. And I honor him for it. This admission of Texas was in 1845. Then, in 1847, *flagrante bello* between the United States and Mexico, the proposition I have mentioned was brought forward by my friend from Georgia, and the Northern Democracy voted straight ahead against it. Their remedy was to apply to the acquisitions, after they should come in, the Wilmot proviso. What follows? These two gentlemen, worthy and honorable and influential men, and if they had not been they could not have carried the measure, these two gentlemen, members of this body, brought in Texas, and by their votes they also prevented the passage of the resolution of the honorable member from Georgia, and then they went home and took the lead in the Free-soil party. And there they stand, sir! They leave us here, bound in honor and conscience by the resolutions of annexation, they leave us here, to take the odium of fulfilling the obligations in favor of slavery, which they voted us into, or else the greater odium of violating those obligations, while they are at home making capital and rousing speeches for free-soil and no slavery. [Laughter.] And, therefore, I say, sir, that there is not a chapter in our history, respecting public measures and public men, more full of what should create surprise, more full of what does create, in my mind, extreme mortification, than that of the conduct of this Northern Democracy.

Mr. President, sometimes, when a man is found in a new relation to things around him and to other men, he says the world has changed, and that he has not changed. I believe, sir, that our self respect leads us often to make this declaration in regard to ourselves, when it is not exactly true. An individual is more apt to change, perhaps, than all the world around him. But, under the present circumstances, and under the responsibility which I know I incur by what I am now stating here, I feel at liberty to recur to the various expressions and statements, made at various times, of my own opinions and resolutions respecting the admission of Texas, and all that has followed. Sir, as early as 1836, or in the earlier part of 1837, there was conversation and correspondence between myself and some private friends, on this project of annexing Texas to the United States; and an honorable gentleman with whom I have had a long acquaintance, a friend of mine, now perhaps in this chamber, I mean Gen. Hamilton, of South Carolina, was knowing to that correspondence. I had voted for the recognition of Texan independence, because I believed it was an existing fact, surprising and astonishing as it was, and I wished well to the new republic: but I manifested from the first utter opposition to bringing her, with her territory, into the Union. I had occasion, sir, in 1837, to meet friends in New York, on some political occasion, and I then stated my sentiments upon the subject. It was the first time that I had occasion to advert to it; and I will ask a friend near me to do me the favor to read an extract from the speech, for the Senate may find it rather tedious to listen to the whole of it. It was delivered in Niblo's Garden in 1837.

Mr. Greene then read the following extract from the speech of Mr. Webster, to which he referred:

"Gentlemen, we all see that, by whomsoever possessed, Texas is likely to be a slaveholding country; and I frankly avow my entire unwillingness to do anything which shall extend the slavery of the African race on this continent, or add other slaveholding States to the Union.

"When I say that I regard slavery in itself as a great moral, social, and political evil, I only use language which has been adopted by distinguished men, themselves citizens of slaveholding States.

"I shall do nothing, therefore, to favor or encourage its further extension. We have slavery already among us. The Constitution found it among us; it recognised it, and gave it solemn guaranties.

"To the full extent of these guaranties, we are all bound in honor, in justice, and by the Constitution. All the stipulations contained in the Constitution in favor of the slaveholding States, which are already in the Union, ought to be fulfilled, and, so far as depends on me, shall be fulfilled in the fulness of their spirit, and to the exactness of their letter. Slavery, as it exists in the States, is beyond the reach of Congress. It is a concern of the States themselves. They have never submitted it to Congress, and Congress has no rightful power over it.

"I shall concur, therefore, in no act, no measure, no menace, no indication of purpose, which shall interfere or threaten to interfere with the exclusive authority of the several States over the subject of slavery, as it exists within their respective limits. All this appears to me to be matter of plain and imperative duty.

"But when we come to speak of admitting new States, the subject assumes an entirely different aspect. Our rights and our duties are then both different. * * *

"I see, therefore, no political necessity for the annexation of Texas to the Union—no advantages to be derived from it; and objections to it of a strong, and, in my judgment, of a decisive character."

Mr. Webster. I have nothing, sir, to add to, nor to take from, those sentiments. That speech, the Senate will perceive, was in 1837. The purpose of immediately annexing Texas at that time was abandoned or postponed; and it was not revived with any vigor for some years. In the meantime it had so happened that I had become a member of the Executive Administration, and was for a short period in the Department of State. The annexation of Texas was a subject of conversation, not confidential, with the President and heads of Departments, as well as with other public men. No serious attempt was then made, however, to bring it about. I left the Department of State in May, 1843, and shortly after I learned, though by means which were no way connected with official information, that a design had been taken up of bringing in Texas, with her slave territory and population, into the United States. I was in Washington at the time, and persons are now here who will remember that we had an arranged meeting for conversation upon it. I went home to Massachusetts and proclaimed the existence of that purpose, but I could get no audience, and but little attention. Some did not believe it, and some were too much engaged in their own pursuits to give it any heed. They had gone to their farms, or to their merchandise, and it was impossible to arouse any sentiments in New England or in Massachusetts that should combine the two great political parties against this annexation; and indeed there was no hope of bringing the Northern Democracy into that view, for the leaning was all the other way. But, sir, even with Whigs, and leading Whigs, I am ashamed to say, there was a great indifference towards the admission of Texas with slave territory into this Union. The project went on. I was then out of Congress. The annexation resolutions passed the 1st of March, 1845; the Legislature of Texas complied with the conditions and accepted the guaranties; for the phraseology of the language of the resolution is, that Texas is to come in "upon the conditions and under the guaranties herein prescribed." I happened to be returned to the Senate in March, 1845, and was here in December, 1845, when the acceptance by Texas of the conditions proposed by Congress were laid before us by the President, and an act for the consummation of the connexion was laid before the two Houses. The connexion was then not completed. A final law doing the deed of annexation ultimately had not been passed; and when it was put upon its final passage here, I expressed my opposition to it, and recorded my vote in the negative; and there that vote stands, with the observations that I made upon that occasion. It has happened that between 1837 and this time, on various occasions and opportunities, I have expressed my entire opposition to the admission of slaves States, or the acquisition of new slave territories, to be added to the United States. I know, sir, no change in my own sentiments or my own purposes in that respect. I will now again ask my friend from Rhode Island to read another extract from a speech of mine, made at a Whig Convention in Springfield, Massachusetts, in the month of September, 1847.

Mr. Greene here read the following extract:

"We hear much just now of a *panacea* for the dangers and evils of slavery and slave annexation, which they call the '*Wilmot proviso.*' That certainly is a just sentiment, but it is not a sentiment to found any new party upon. It is not a sentiment on which Massachusetts Whigs differ. There is not a man in this hall who holds to it more firmly than I do, nor one who adheres to it more than another.

"I feel some little interest in this matter, sir. Did not I commit myself in 1837 to the whole doctrine, fully, entirely? And I must be permitted to say that I cannot quite consent that more recent discoverers should claim the merit and take out a patent.

"I deny the priority of their invention. Allow me to say, sir, it is not their thunder." * *

"We are to use the first and last and every occasion which offers to oppose the extension of slave power.

"But I speak of it here, as in Congress, as a political question, a question for statesmen to act upon. We must so regard it. I certainly do not mean to say that it is less important in a moral point of view, that it is not more important in many other points of view; but, as a legislator, or in any official capacity, I must look at it, consider it, and decide it as a matter of political action."

Mr. Webster. On other occasions, in debates here, I have expressed my determination to vote for no acquisition, or cession, or annexation, North or South, East or West. My opinion has been, that we have territory enough, and that we should follow the Spartan maxim, "improve, adorn what you have, seek no further." I think that it was in some observations that I made here on the three million loan bill, that I avowed that sentiment. In short, sir, the sentiment has been avowed quite as often, in as many places, and before as many assemblies, as any humble sentiments of mine ought to be avowed.

But now, that, under certain conditions, Texas is in, with all her territories, as a slave State, with a solemn pledge, also, that if she shall be divided into many States, those States may come in as slave States south of 36° 30′, how are we to deal with this subject? I know no way of honest legislation, when the proper time comes for the enactment, but to carry into effect all that we have stipulated to do. I do not entirely agree with my honorable friend from Tennessee, (Mr. Bell,) that, as soon as the time comes when she is entitled to another representative, we should create a new State. The rule in regard to it I take to be this: that, when we have created new States out of Territories, we have generally gone upon the idea that when there is population enough to form a State, sixty thousand or some such thing, we would create a State; but it is quite a different thing when a State is divided, and two or more States made out of it. It does not follow, in such a case, that the same rule of apportionment should be applied. That, however, is a matter for the consideration of Congress, when the proper time arrives. I may not then be here. I may have no vote to give on the occasion, but I wish it to be distinctly understood, to-day, that, according to my view of the matter, this Government is solemnly pledged, by law and contract, to create new States out of Texas, with her consent, when her population shall justify such a proceeding, and so far as such States are formed out of Texan territory lying south of 36° 30′, to let them come in as slave States. That is the meaning of the resolution which our friends, the Northern Democracy, have left us to fulfil; and I, for one, mean to fulfil it, because I will not violate the faith of the Government. What I mean to say is, that the time for the admission of new States formed out of Texas, the number of such States, their boundaries, and the requisite amounts of population, and other things connected with the admission, are in the free discretion of Congress, except this, to wit, that when new States, formed out of Texas, are to be admitted, they have a right, by legal stipulation and contract, to come in as slave States.

Now, as to California and New Mexico, I hold slavery to be excluded from those Territories by a law, even superior to that which admits and sanctions it in Texas. I mean the law of nature, of physical geography, the law of the formation of the earth. That law settles forever, with a strength beyond all terms of human enactment, that slavery cannot exist in California or New Mexico. Understand me, sir; I mean slavery as we regard it; slaves in gross, of the colored race, transferable by sale and delivery, like other property. I shall not discuss the point, but leave it to the learned gentlemen who have undertaken to discuss it; but I suppose there is no slave of that description in California now. I understand that *peonism*, a sort of penal servitude, exists there, or rather a sort of voluntary sale of a man and his offspring for debt, as it is arranged and exists in some parts of California and Mexico. But what I mean to say is, that African slavery, as we see it among us, is as utterly impossible to find itself, or to be found in Mexico, as any other natural impossibility. California and New Mexico are Asiatic, in their formation and scenery. They are composed of vast ridges of mountains of enormous height, with broken ridges and deep valleys. The sides of these mountains are barren, entirely barren; their tops capped by perrenial snow. There may be in California, now made free by its constitution, and no doubt there are, some tracts of valuable land. But it is not so in New Mexico. Pray, what is the evidence which every gentleman must have obtained on this subject, from information sought by himself, or communicated by others. I have inquired and read all I could find, in order to obtain information on this important question. What is there in New Mexico that could by any possibility induce any body to go there with slaves? There are some narrow strips of tillable land on the borders of the rivers; but the rivers themselves dry up, before midsummer is gone. All that the people can do in that region, isto raise some little articles, some little wheat for their tortillas, and all that by irrigation. And who expects to see a hundred black men cultivating tobacco, corn, cotton, rice, or any thing else, on lands in New Mexico, made fertile only by irrigation? I look upon it, therefore, as a fixed fact, to use an expression current at this day, that both California and New Mexico are destined to be free, so far as they are settled at all, which I believe, especially in regard to New Mexico, will be very little for a great length of time; free by the arrangement of things by the Power above us. I have therefore to say, in this respect also, that this country is fixed for freedom, to as many persons as shall ever live in it by as irrepealable and more irrepealable a law, than the law that attaches to the right of holding slaves in Texas; and I will say further, that if a resolution, or a law, were now before us to provide a territorial Government for New Mexico, I would not vote to put any prohibition into it whatever. The use of such a prohibition would be idle, as it respects any effect it would have upon the Territory; and I would not take pains to re-affirm an ordinance of Nature, nor to re-enact the will of God. And I would put in no Wilmot proviso for the purpose of a taunt or a reproach. I would put into it no evidence of the votes of superior power, for no purpose but to wound the pride, even whether a just pride, a rational pride, or an irrational pride, to wound the pride of the gentlemen who belong to Southern States. I have no such object, no such purpose. They would think it a taunt, an indignity; they would think it to be an act taking away from them what they regard a proper equality of privilege; and whether they expect to realize any benefit from it or not, they would think it a theoretic wrong; that something more or less derogatory to their character and their rights had taken place. I propose to inflict no such wound upon any body, unless something essentially important to the country, and efficient to the preservation of liberty and freedom, is to be effected. Therefore, I repeat, sir, and I repeat it because I wish it to be understood, that I do not propose to address the Senate often on this subject. I desire to pour out all my heart in as plain a manner as possible; and I say, again, that if a proposition were now here for a Government for New Mexico, and it was moved to insert a provision for a prohibition of slavery, I would not vote for it.

Now, Mr. President, I have established, so far as I proposed to go into any line of observation to ablish, the proposition with which I set out, and upon which I propose to stand or fall; and that that the whole territory of the States in the United States, or in the newly acquired territory of the iited States, has a fixed and settled character, now fixed and settled by law, which cannot be repealed the case of Texas without a violation of public faith, and cannot be repealed by any human power regard to California or New Mexico; that, under one or other of these laws, every foot of territory the States or in the Territories has now received a fixed and decided character.

Sir, if we were now making a Government for New Mexico, and any body should propose a Wilot proviso, I should treat it exactly as Mr. Polk treated that provision for excluding slavery from egon. Mr. Polk was known to be in opinion decidedly averse to the Wilmot proviso; but he felt e necessity of establishing a government for the Territory of Oregon, and, though the proviso was ere, he knew it would be entirely nugatory; and, since it must be entirely nugatory, since it took ay no right, no describable, no estimable, no weighable or tangible right of the South, he said he ould sign the bill for the sake of enacting a law to form a government in that Territory, and let that tirely useless, and, in that connexion entirely senseless, proviso remain. For myself, I will say at we hear much of the annexation of Canada; and if there be any man, any of the Northern Demoacy, or any one of the Free-Soil party, who supposes it necessary to insert a Wilmot proviso in a rritorial government for New Mexico, that man will of course be of opinion that it is necessary to otect the everlasting snows of Canada from the foot of slavery by the same overspreading wing of an t of Congress. Sir, wherever there is a particular good to be done; wherever there is a foot of land be staid back from becoming slave territory, I am ready to assert the principle of the exclusion of avery. I am pledged to it from the year 1837; I have been pledged to it again and again; and I will rform those pledges; but I will not do a thing unnecessary, that wounds the feelings of others, or at does disgrace to my own understanding.

Mr. President, in the excited times in which we live, there is found to exist a state of crimination d recrimination between the North and South. There are lists of grievances produced by each; and ose grievances, real or supposed, alienate the minds of one portion of the country from the other, asperate the feelings, subdue the sense of fraternal affection, patriotic love and mutual regard. shall bestow a little attention, sir, upon these various grievances produced on the one side, and on the her. I begin with the complaints of the South. I will not answer, further than I have, the general atements of the honorable Senator from South Carolina, that the North has grown upon the South consequence of the manner of administering this Government, in the collecting of its revenues, and forth. These are disputed topics, and I have no inclination to enter into them. But I will state ese complaints, especially one complaint of the South, which has in my opinion just foundation; d that is, that there has been found at the North, among individuals and among the legislators of the orth, a disinclination to perform, fully, their constitutional duties in regard to the return of persons und to service who have escaped into the free States. In that respect, it is my judgment that the outh is right, and the North is wrong. Every member of every Northern Legislature is bound by th, like every other officer in the country, to support the Constitution of the United States; and this ticle of the Constitution, which says to these States they shall deliver up fugitives from service, is as nding in honor and conscience as any other article. No man fulfils his duty in any Legislature who ts himself to find excuses, evasions, escapes from this constitutional obligation. I have always ought that the Constitution addressed itself to the Legislatures of the States themselves, or to the ates themselves. It says that those persons escaping to other States shall be delivered up, and I nfess I have always been of the opinion that it was an injunction upon the States themselves. When is said that a person escaping into another State, and becoming therefore within the jurisdiction of at State, shall be delivered up, it seems to me the import of the passage is, that the State itself, in edience to the Constitution, shall cause him to be delivered up. That is my judgment. I have alays entertained that opinion, and I entertain it now. But when the subject, some years ago, was fore the Supreme Court of the United States, the majority of the judges held that the power to cause gitives from service to be delivered up was a power to be exercised under the authority of this Govnment. I do not know, on the whole, that it may not have been a fortunate decision. My habit is respect the result of judicial deliberations and the solemnity of judicial decisions. But, as it now ands, the business of seeing that these fugitives are delivered up resides in the power of Congress and e national judicature, and my friend at the head of the Judiciary Committee has a bill on the subject ow before the Senate, with some amendments to it, which I propose to support, with all its provions, to the fullest extent. And I desire to call the attention of all sober-minded men, of all consciens men, in the North, of all men who are not carried away by any fanatical idea or by any false idea hatever, to their constitutional obligations. I put it to all the sober and sound minds at the North as question of morals and a question of conscience. What right have they, in their legislative capacity, any other, to endeavor to get round this Constitution, to embarrass the free exercise of the rights cured by the Constitution to the persons whose slaves escape from them? None at all; none at all. either in the forum of conscience, nor before the face of the Constitution, are they justified, in my inion. Of course it is a matter for their consideration. They probably, in the turmoil of the times, ave not stopped to consider of this; they have followed what seems to be the current of thought and motives as the occasion arose, and they neglected to investigate fully the real question, and to conder their constitutional obligations; as I am sure, if they did consider, they would fulfil them with acrity. Therefore, I repeat, sir, that here is a ground of complaint against the North well founded, hich ought to be removed, which it is now in the power of the different departments of this Government to remove; which calls for the enactment of proper laws authorizing the judicature of this ernment, in the several States, to do all that is necessary for the recapture of fugitive slaves, an the restoration of them to those who claim them. Wherever I go, and whenever I speak on the ject, and when I speak here I desire to speak to the whole North, I say that the South has be jured in this respect, and has a right to complain; and the North has been too careless of what I the Constitution peremptorily and emphatically enjoins upon it as a duty.

Complaint has been made against certain resolutions that emanate from Legislatures at the N and are sent here to us, not only on the subject of slavery in this District, but sometimes recomn ing Congress to consider the means of abolishing slavery in the States. I should be sorry to be upon to present any resolutions here which could not be referrable to any committee or any pow Congress; and, therefore, I should be unwilling to receive from the Legislature of Massachusett instructions to present resolutions expressive of any opinion whatever on the subject of slavery as exists at the present moment in the States, for two reasons: because, first, I do not consider th Legislature of Massachusetts has any thing to do with it; and next, I do not consider that I, as her r sentative here, have any thing to do with it. Sir, it has become, in my opinion, quite too common; if the Legislatures of the States do not like that opinion, they have a great deal more power to put it d than I have to uphold it; it has become, in my opinion, quite too common a practice for the State L latures to present resolutions here on all subjects, and to instruct us here on all subjects. There public man that requires instruction more than I do, or who requires information more than I d desires it more heartily; but I do not like to have it come in too imperative a shape. I took n with pleasure, of some remarks upon this subject made the other day in the Senate of Massachu by a young man of talent and character, of whom the best hopes may be entertained. I mean Hillard. He told the Senate of Massachusetts that he would vote for no instructions whatever forwarded to members of Congress, nor for any resolutions to be offered, expressive of the sen Massachusetts, as to what her members of Congress ought to do. He said that he saw no prop in one set of public servants giving instructions and reading lectures to another set of public serv To their own master all of them must stand or fall, and that master is their constituents. I wish sentiments could become more common, a great deal more common. I have never entered int question, and never shall, about the binding force of instructions. I will, however, simply say if there be any matter of interest pending in this body, while I am a member of it, in which M chusetts has an interest of her own not adverse to the general interests of the country, I shall p her instructions with gladness of heart, and with all the efficiency which I can bring to the occa But if the question be one which affects her interest, and at the same time affects the interests of all States, I shall no more regard her political wishes or instructions than I would regard the wishes man who might appoint me an arbitrator, or referee, to decide some question of important private and who might *instruct* me to decide in his favor. If ever there was a Government upon earth, it is Government; if ever there was a body upon earth, it is this body, which should consider itse composed by agreement of all, each member appointed by some, but organized by the general co of all, sitting here under the solemn obligations of oath and conscience to do that which they thi be best for the good of the whole.

Then, sir, there are the abolition societies, of which I am unwilling to speak, but in regard to w I have very clear notions and opinions. I do not think them useful. I think their operations fo last twenty years have produced nothing good or valuable. At the same time, I know thousan their members are honest and good men; perfectly well meaning men. They have excited feel they think they must do something for the cause of liberty, and in their sphere of action they d seewhat else they can do, than to contribute to an abolition press, or an abolition society, or to pa abolition lecturer. I do not mean to impute gross motives even to the leaders of these societies, am not blind to the consequences. I cannot but see what mischiefs their interference with the S has produced. And is it not plain to every man? Let any gentleman who doubts of that, rec the debates in the Virginia House of Delegates in 1832, and he will see with what freedom a pro tion made by Mr. Randolph for the gradual abolition of slavery was discussed in that body. E one spoke of slavery as he thought; very ignominious and disparaging names and epithets wer plied to it. The debates in the House of Delegates on that occasion, I believe, were all publis They were read by every colored man who could read, and if there were any who could not those debates were read to them by others. At that time Virginia was not unwilling nor afrai discuss this question, and to let that part of her population know as much of it as they could l That was in 1832. As has been said by the honorable member from South Carolina, these abol societies commenced their course of action in 1835. It is said, I do not know how true it may be, they sent incendiary publications into the slave States; at any event, they attempted to arouse, an arouse, a very strong feeling; in other words, they created great agitation in the North against S ern slavery. Well, what was the result? The bonds of the slaves were bound more firmly before; their rivets were more strongly fastened. Public opinion, which in Virginia had begun exhibited against slavery, and was opening out for the discussion of the question, drew back and itself up in its castle. I wish to know whether any body in Virginia can, now, talk as Mr. Rand Gov. McDowell, and others talked there, openly, and sent their remarks to the press, in 1832? all know the fact, and we all know the cause; and every thing that this agitating people have don been, not to enlarge, but to restrain, not to set free, but to bind faster the slave population of the S That is my judgment. Sir, as I have said, I know many abolitionists in my own neighborhood, honest, good people, misled, as I think, by strange enthusiasm; but they wish to do someth and they are called on to contribute, and they do contribute; and it is my firm opinion this day, the last twenty years as much money has been collected and paid to the abolition societies, on presses, and abolition lecturers, as would purchase the freedom of every slave, man, woman, ild in the State of Maryland, and send them all to Liberia. I have no doubt of it. But I have learn that the benevolence of these abolition societies has at any time taken that particular turn. hter.]

in, sir, the violence of the press is complained of. The press violent! Why, sir, the press is t every where. There are outrageous reproaches in the North against the South, and there eproaches no better in the South against the North. Sir, the extremists of both parts country are violent; they mistake loud and violent talk for eloquence and for reason. They that he who talks loudest reasons best. And this we must expect, when the press is free, is here, and I trust always will be, for, with all its licentiousness, and all its evil, the and absolute freedom of the press is essential to the preservation of government on the basis of constitution. Wherever it exists, there will be foolish paragraphs and violent paragraphs in ess, as there are, I am sorry to say, foolish speeches and violent speeches in both Houses of ess. In truth, sir, I must say that, in my opinion, the vernacular tongue of the country has e greatly vitiated, depraved, and corrupted by the style of our congressional debates. [Laugh- And if it were possible for our debates in Congress to vitiate the principles of the people as as they have depraved their taste, I should cry out, "God save the Republic!"

ll, in all this I see no solid grievance, no grievance presented by the South, within the redress Government, but the single one to which I have referred; and that is, the want of a proper to the injunction of the Constitution for the delivery of fugitive slaves.

re are also complaints of the North against the South. I need not go over them particularly. st and gravest is, that the North adopted the Constitution, recognising the existence of slavery States, and recognising the right, to a certain extent, of representation of the slaves in Congress, a state of sentiment and expectation, which do not now exist; and that, by events, by circum-, by the eagerness of the South to acquire territory and extend her slave population, the North self, in regard to the influence of the South and the North, of the free States and the slave States, it never did expect to find itself when they agreed to the compact of the Constitution. They com- herefore, that, instead of slavery being regarded as an evil, as it was then, an evil which all would be extinguished gradually, it is now regarded by the South as an institution to be cher- nd preserved, and extended; an institution which the South has already extended to the ut- heir power by the acquisition of new territory.

l, then, passing from that, every body in the North reads; and every body reads whatsoever wspapers contain; and the newspapers, some of them, especially those presses to which I luded, are careful to spread about among the people every reproachful sentiment uttered by uthern man bearing at all against the North; every thing that is calculated to exasperate, ate; and there are many such things, as every body will admit, from the South, or some of it, which are spread abroad among the reading people; and they do exasperate, and , and produce a most mischievous effect upon the public mind at the North. Sir, I would ice things of this sort appearing in obscure quarters; but one thing has occurred in this which struck me very forcibly. An honorable member from Louisiana addressed us the ay on this subject. I suppose there is not a more amiable and worthy gentleman in this r, nor a gentleman who would be more slow to give offence to any body, and he did not mean emarks to give offence. But what did he say? Why, sir, he took pains to run a contrast be- he slaves of the South and the laboring people of the North, giving the preference in all points ition, and comfort, and happiness, to the slaves of the South. The honorable member, doubt- l not suppose that he gave any offence, or did any injustice. He was merely expressing his But does he know how remarks of that sort will be received by the laboring people of the Why, who are the laboring people of the North? They are the North. They are the peo- cultivate their own farms with their own hands; freeholders, educated men, independent men. say, sir, that five-sixths of the whole property of the North is in the hands of the laborers of th; they cultivate their farms, they educate their children, they provide the means of inde- e; if they are not freeholders, they earn wages; these wages accumulate, are turned into cap- new freeholds, and small capitalists are created. That is the case, and such the course of mong the industrious and frugal. And what can these people think when so respectable and a gentleman as the member from Louisiana undertakes to prove that the absolute ignorance and ct slavery of the South are more in conformity with the high purposes and destiny of immortal, human beings, than the educated, the independent, free labor of the North?

is a more tangible and irritating cause of grievance at the North. Free blacks are constantly d in the vessels of the North, generally as cooks or stewards. When the vessel arrives, at a n port, these free colored men are taken on shore, by the police or municipal authority, impri- nd kept in prison, till the vessel is again ready to sail. This is not only irritating, but exceed- justifiable and oppressive. Mr. Hoar's mission, some time ago, to South Carolina, was a nded effort to remove this cause of complaint. The North thinks such imprisonments illegal onstitutional; as the cases occur constantly, and frequently, they think it a great grievance.

sir, so far as any of these grievances have their foundation in matters of law, they can be re- and ought to be redressed; and so far as they have their foundation in matters of opinion, in it, in mutual crimination and recrimination, all that we can do is to endeavor to allay the , and cultivate a better feeling and more fraternal sentiments between the South and the North. resident, I should much prefer to have heard from every member on this floor declarations of opinion that this Union should never be dissolved, than the declaration of opinion that, in any ca under the pressure of any circumstances, such a dissolution was possible. I hear with pain, a anguish, and distress, the word secession, especially when it falls from the lips of those who are e nently patriotic, and known to the country, and known all over the world, for their political servic Secession! Peaceable secession! Sir, your eyes and mine are never destined to see that mirac The dismemberment of this vast country without convulsion! The breaking up of the fountains the great deep without ruffling the surface! Who is so foolish, I beg every body's pardon, as to pect to see any such thing? Sir, he who sees these States, now revolving in harmony around a co mon centre, and expects to see them quit their places and fly off without convulsion, may look next hour to see the heavenly bodies rush from their spheres, and jostle against each other in the rea of space, without causing the crush of the universe. There can be no such thing as a peaceable cession. Peaceable secession is an utter impossibility. Is the great Constitution under which we here, covering this whole country, is it to be thawed and melted away by secession, as the sn on the mountain melt under the influence of a vernal sun? disappear almost unobserved, and die No, sir! No, sir! I will not state what might produce the disruption of the States; but, sir, I se as plainly as I see the sun in heaven, I see that disruption must produce such a war as I will describe, *in its twofold character*.

Peaceable secession!—peaceable secession! The concurrent agreement of all the members of great republic to separate! A voluntary separation, with alimony on one side and on the other. W what would be the result? Where is the line to be drawn? What States are to secede? What is remain American? What am I to be? An American no longer? Where is the flag of the repu to remain? Where is the eagle still to tower? or is he to cower and shrink and fall to the grou Why, sir, our ancestors—our fathers and our grandfathers, those of them that are yet living amo us with prolonged lives, would rebuke and reproach us; and our children and our grandchildren wo cry out shame upon us, if we, of this generation, should dishonor these ensigns of the power of Government and the harmony of the Union, which is every day felt among us with so much joy gratitude. What is to become of the army? What is to become of the navy? What is to becom the public lands? How is each of the thirty States to defend itself? I know, although the idea not been stated distinctly, there is to be a Southern Confederacy. I do not mean, when I allud this statement, that any one seriously contemplates such a state of things. I do not mean to say it is true, but I have heard it suggested elsewhere, that that idea has originated a design to sepa I am sorry, sir, that it has ever been thought of, talked of, or dreamed of, in the wildest flight human imagination. But the idea must be of a separation, including the slave States upon one and the free States on the other. Sir, there is not, I may express myself too strongly, perhaps, some things, some moral things, are almost as impossible as other natural or physical things; a hold the idea of a separation of these States, those that are free to form one government and those are slaveholding to form another, as a moral impossibility. We could not separate the States by such line, if we were to draw it. We could not sit down here to-day and draw a line of separ that would satisfy any five men in the country. There are natural causes that would keep and t together, and there are social and domestic relations which we could not break if we would, and w we should not if we could. Sir, nobody can look over the face of this country at the present mor nobody can see where its population is the most dense and growing, without being ready to ac and compelled to admit, that ere long America will be in the valley of the Mississippi.

Well, now, sir, I beg to inquire what the wildest enthusiast has to say on the possibility of cu off that river and leaving free States at its source, and its branches, and slave States down ne mouth? Pray, sir; pray, sir, let me say to the people of this country that these things are wort their pondering and of their consideration. Here, sir, are five millions of freemen in the free S north of the river Ohio: can any body suppose that this population can be severed by a line tha vides them from the territory of a foreign and an alien Government, down somewhere, the Lord k where, upon the lower banks of the Mississippi? What would become of Missouri? Will sh the arrondissement of the slave States? Shall the man from the Yellow Stone and the Platte be nected, in the new Republic, with the man who lives on the southern extremity of the Cape of Fle Sir, I am ashamed to pursue this line of remark. I dislike it, I have an utter disgust for it. I w rather hear of natural blasts and mildews, war, pestilence, and famine, than to hear gentlemen ta secession. To break up! to break up this great Government, to dismember this great country, to ast Europe with an act of folly such as Europe for two centuries has never beheld in any Governm No, sir; no sir! There will be no secession. Gentlemen are not serious when they talk of seces

Sir, I hear there is to be a Convention held at Nashville. I am bound to believe that if worthy tlemen meet at Nashville in convention, their object will be to adopt counsels conciliatory, to a the South to forbearance and moderation, and to advise the North to forbearance and moderatio to inculcate principles of brotherly love and affection, and attachment to the Constitution of the co as it now is. I believe, if the Convention meet at all, it will be for this purpose; for certainly, i meet for any purpose hostile to the Union, they have been singularly inappropriate in their sel of a place. I remember, sir, that when the treaty was concluded between France and England, peace of Amiens, a stern old Englishman and an orator, who disliked the terms of the peace as minious to England, said in the House of Commons, that if King William could know the te that treaty, he would turn in his coffin. Let me commend this saying of Mr. Windham, in all i phasis and in all its force, to any persons who shall meet at Nashville for the purpose of conc measures for the overthrow of the Union over the bones of Andrew Jackson.

Sir, I wish now to make two remarks, and hasten to a conclusion. I wish to say, in regard to T that if it should be, hereafter, at any time, the pleasure of the Government of Texas to cede to the United States a portion, larger or smaller, of her territory which lies adjacent to New Mexico, and north of 34° of north latitude, to be formed into free States, for a fair equivalent in money or in the payment of her debt, I think it an object well worthy the consideration of Congress, and I shall be happy to concur in it myself, if I should be in the public counsels of the country at the time.

I have one other remark to make. In my observations upon slavery as it has existed in the country, and as it now exists, I have expressed no opinion of the mode of its extinguishment or melioration. I will say, however, though I have nothing to propose on that subject, because I do not deem myself so competent as other gentlemen to consider it, that if any gentleman from the South shall propose a scheme of colonization, to be carried on by this Government upon a large scale, for the transportation of free colored people to any colony or any place in the world, I should be quite disposed to incur almost any degree of expense to accomplish that object. Nay, sir, following an example set here more than twenty years ago by a great man, then a Senator from New York, I would return to Virginia, and through her for the benefit of the whole South, the money received from the lands and territories ceded by her to this Government, for any such purpose as to relieve, in whole or in part, or in any way to diminish or deal beneficially with, the free colored population of the Southern States. I have said that I honor Virginia for her cession of this territory. There have been received into the treasury of the United States eighty millions of dollars, the proceeds of the sales of the public lands ceded by her. If the residue should be sold at the same rate, the whole aggregate will exceed two hundred millions of dollars. If Virginia and the South see fit to adopt any proposition to relieve themselves from the free people of color among them, they have my free consent that the Government shall pay them any sum of money out of its proceeds, which may be adequate to the purpose.

And now, Mr. President, I draw these observations to a close. I have spoken freely, and I meant to do so. I have sought to make no display; I have sought to enliven the occasion by no animated discussion, nor have I attempted any train of elaborate argument. I have wished only to speak my sentiments, fully and at large, being desirous once and for all to let the Senate know, and to let the country know, the opinions and sentiments which I entertain on all these subjects. These opinions are not likely to be suddenly changed. If there be any future service that I can render to the country, consistently with these sentiments and opinions, I shall cheerfully render it. If there be not, I shall still be glad to have had an opportunity to disburden my conscience from the bottom of my heart, and to make known every political sentiment that therein exists.

And now, Mr. President, instead of speaking of the possibility or utility of secession, instead of dwelling in these caverns of darkness, instead of groping with those ideas so full of all that is horrid and horrible, let us come out into the light of day; let us enjoy the fresh air of Liberty and Union; let us cherish those hopes which belong to us; let us devote ourselves to those great objects that are fit for our consideration and our action; let us raise our conceptions to the magnitude and the importance of the duties that devolve upon us; let our comprehension be as broad as the country for which we act, our aspirations as high as its certain destiny; let us not be pigmies in a case that calls for men. Never did there devolve on any generation of men higher trusts than now devolve upon us, for the preservation of this Constitution, and the harmony and peace of all who are destined to live under it. Let us make our generation one of the strongest, and the brightest link in that golden chain, which is destined, I fondly believe, to grapple the people of all the States to this Constitution, for ages to come. It is a great, popular, constitutional Government, guarded by law, and by judicature, and defended by the whole affections of the people. No monarchial throne presses these States together; no iron chain of despotic power encircles them; they live and stand upon a Government popular in its form, representative in its character, founded upon principles of equality, and calculated, we hope, to last forever. In all its history it has been beneficent; it has trodden down no man's liberty; it has crushed no State. Its daily respiration is liberty and patriotism; its yet youthful veins are full of enterprise, courage, and honorable love of glory and renown. Large before, the country has now, by recent events, become vastly larger. This republic now extends, with a vast breadth, across the whole continent. The two great seas of the world wash the one and the other shore. We realize, on a mighty scale, the beautiful description of the ornamental edging of the buckler of Achilles—

"Now the broad shield complete, the artist crowned
With his last band, and poured the ocean round;
In living silver seemed the waves to roll,
And beat the buckler's verge, and bound the whole."

www.ingramcontent.com/pod-product-compliance
Lightning Source LLC
LaVergne TN
LVHW020643110826
845149LV00004B/1342

* 9 7 8 1 4 1 8 1 9 0 1 7 0 *